beautifully alien refraction

miriam e. walsh

book 1: random series

ardornata
publishing

Cover art by Miriam E. Walsh
Book design by Miriam E. Walsh

ISBN 978-0-9836598-0-8

ardornata publishing
www.ardornatadesign.com

Table of Contents

About The Author

Miriam E. Walsh has worn many hats to pay the bills:
mental health worker at a detox unit, drafter in the engineering field
and graphic designer --- but she has always donned the hat of a
poet.

For many years, at her home on the south shore in Massachusetts,
she has tended to many writing projects, the culmination of which
is the Random Series of books.These poems have been written in
many places; lunch breaks, poetry readings, train rides and, yes,
car rides!

She has been published in U.M.Ph.! Prose Online and is a regular
fixture at local poetry venues including "Poetry: The Art Of Words
Mike Amado Memorial Series" in Plymouth, Massachusetts.

Miriam E. Walsh has an BS Degree in Psychology from
Bridgewater State College, where she also minored in art. She is
an accomplished photographer/visual artist and a member of the
Plymouth Arts Guild.

random series
book 1 : beautifully alien refraction
book 2 : primitive awe
book 3 : forced continuity
book 4 : small lucidities

the sentinel and the sentiment 92

(a poem for two voices)

standing,   flowing,

brooding,   knowing,

my face behooving   reflection showing

all who gape   all who wade

before me   through me

i mark a place, i am not a place

a time   a time   a time

i must protect   i am a protection

with my   without

stone-cold constancy.   a logic consistency.

a mystery   a truth

on the vastness,   in the sublimeness,

an imposition   clear moment

of composition   in the torrent

by one fateful,   of one hateful,

forgetful being.   regretful being.

i cannot die;

only a remnant   only the essence

of one once alive.   of the whole alive

a shell   an opal

marking   glistening

guarding listening

forgotten secrets   memory's music

and   on

primoridial fears.   immortal ears.

(infinity) 95

every hour
passes slowly as the film reels
of a senseless slaughter
and each minute dies-----cold on the pavement,
and i alone
kneel and grieve
over the body.
while watches have appointments to make
and feet have clerical destinies to take
and streetlamps
make us forget
that evening ever comes.
holding its hand
raising its lips
to breathe time's last words:
the lover's bed.
the smoky halls
of a cafe's conversation potentiality.
the first glance,
the last glimpses.
the moment slowly dies;
it smiles up at my acknowledgment.
as legs shuffle passed
my illegal, naked sentimentality,
to be ignored and unencouraged
as a beggar's cup.
and my fingers, empty now,
but stained to my skin
my eyes
and further within.
walking wardrobes
with their priorities
shoulder and shove
with schedules as securities
that there will always be time------- later.
as i wait; breathing softly,
the scent---
of the next murder.

two samurais 94

two samurais
in a reigning night
still, standing
steel to stealth.
you will not enter
my door,
i will not exit
my life;
and we stare,
begging silently
stain glass eyes
color your worlds

as brick and fire
terminate my growth.
open as questions,
closed as expectations.
the first to move
is the first to die.
lovers afraid to love
become
warriors practicing strategy
within a tragedy
two samurais.
soul to soul
steel to steel.

complements 94

she is sun,
i am night.
dawn and dusk,
mesh together
in perfect unity.
sun
golden glitter rays,
summer,blue sky eyes
moon
pale fragility
within swirling night
stars piercing black,eyes.
within and without
we flow.
gapless
in the interwoven scheme.
what one lacks
the other fills.
what one needs
the other provides.
polarity to perfection
sun
night
could not exist
without each other.

empathy with the storm 94

the clouds crack , bleeding
metabolized to rage,
with neither origin nor
destination.
a flash in my eyes.
a flash that dims days,
electrifies nights;
threatens to break the
windows
of my hospice,
and receive its consummation
in midnights with me.
we both explode
against the randomness
that created us.
your voice
the madness of loneliness
to be so
pure,cleansing
overpowering
but to have no equal.
so as to your raging grief,
no one answers;
no face nor voice like your own.

the ragged clumsy
sheath that holds me
allows me only one voice,
not a composition of
streaming murmurs
whispering chatter
and white hot eternal clatter.
a symphony of
cacophony in every sentence.
poetry
dropping from the vast body
of cloud frenzy and lightning
touching with endless rivulet fingertips
that kidnap me to the cycle, to the storm.
and we almost join
to escape what we are and must be.

two storms that never last too long.

shadow 94

as ebony upon the night
solid yet indistinguishable
there you are;
convulsing with the
sky-land's
enigmatic tides;
yet you are real.
only blatant sun allows me to deny you
as my servant,my train bearer
but as sun surrenders to night
i must surrender to you
the intimacy of strangers,
estranged in embrace;
we are blooms of a familiar root.
when i am warm
you shiver and lengthen
as my eternal reveries.
faceless,unknown eyes;
voiceless,only dancing gestures
to my words.
i fear you
but cannot recede
from your stalking dedication
to your creator,
whose existence is
just as mutual;
for what day dares to abandon
its night
or i,
my shadow.

sole system   94

you are the sun
i, a planet encircling
magnetized to your presence
but distant
to save myself,
and the creatures that inhabit
me.
cycling growth
i lose nothing i create
deathless
with the efficiency of storms
and the fluency of wind.
night and day
turning every facet to you,
feeding hungry terrains.
alive self sufficiency
but
dependent on the brilliant
touch
that caresses, yet never
enough.
we are alone in the infinite
sooner
falling into each other
burning
than slip away
to the dark.

temple   95

lungs scream
as a bird of pray
and in my temple

i am running short on candles,

as those lit wicks
sputter,
drowning
in the pools
of their own baptism.

as windless gusts,
words must extinguish
the flame that they explain
and books read
as sunday's obituaries.

"she lived,she loved, she died"

she was explained away.
she began to die
the moment she murmured
"mama"
and spoke until
she garbled meaningless
the last images of identity.

pain is our poetic imagery.
commas as our beds,
periods as our graves.
a thought once spoken,
a candle ignited,
becomes the center
of its own night.

the icelands   95

the towers scrape the sky
and yet it does not bleed.
in this land there is only snow
as the last gentle hands
settling frozen as indifference,
              on the faces
              of failed summits;
              on the bare arms
              of leafless legions;
              blinding the thoughts
              of the nomads
              to this region.
and through the storm
they pass in silence;
pigments on the white,
angels unable to alight,
for empty burdens
are their obligation
to those who have passed before,
through the storm.
through the storm.
and with the emptiness they build
rooms without content,
words without meaning;
only places for the snow to dwell
only reasons for their hands to swell.
              arms strain ,
              limbs falter;
              and still the landscape
              does not alter.
              spring infants silent,
              aged passed fall,
              and still no substance
              to it all.
and the snow consumes it all with ease;
for in the icelands
what else is there
but to freeze?

the desert   95

the only green
in the desert.
surrounded by
a dry, waterless wasteland
that disguises itself
in its natural crimson
and sandy painterly
splendor.

almost seems
nurturing
but lonely
to solely green.
green
that needs the water
the desert cannot offer;
requires temperance
but granted only
rock-singeing days,
life-freezing nights.

i am the desert.
a mind extending
as immeasurable horizons,
a red sky surrounding,
a barren land unending.
a place of extremes:
sun anger
ice sorrow.

i am no place
for green to grow.

narcissus 95

i washed back the ringlets of your hair
as fingers strumming gently the ripples
of a black,deep , unending pond.
yet still, it streamed through my fingers
making elusive and dancing
the face that seemed mine
but yet its complement.
we are as nymphs to each other
staring into each other's world
as separate unattainable universes;
each other's mythology,
we search meaning in each other.
water nymph
touches
earth nymph,
but only along the boundaries.

and so we stare into each other
wondering

which of us
is
narcissus.

glucose adonis   95

your muscles instigate to be the iris of my eye
with the stillness of a tree, desperate height
you seek the molecules of my attention.
an oak against the sun
claiming it as your cloak.

yet in your rootedness you dance
as if nights demons are at your dorsal
they are your energies
dictating your branches,
whose form you deny as your desire,
orchestrated fences upon the sky.

and with a single frost
your emergencies begin.
you grow and store
but refuse to release the blossoms
and simply sing them on the wind.

mondrian's tree
you abstract into elusiveness.
until the brushstrokes of your worlds
have the frenzied summer haze
of a glucose adonis.

answer to prayer   95

and there is a sun's life
between us
your neck arched upward,
and as my own,
i felt its scream
as a blazing canopy
snd a scything glass floor
that cut the void
into two infinities.

i saw it die.

and on the small blue planet
you saw its echo,
traced in your comfortable sleep,
the shape of an eternal star
as a reference of purpose;
molecular silk
tethering adam to atom,
probability to answer;
secure that there was
a horizon for every star
and a stargazer for every horizon,
and crickets sing
on even a lifeless moon.
and above,below
and around,within;
i see the angles of dimension
while in dementia
you stood;
masters of anthills
watching
the appropriate appropriating
so intent on insects
as soldiers, and me
as father.
must all have arms, legs
and motivation with you?

for you
must there be saviors
to die?

and even as you pray,
your neck arched up-
ward,
your voice begging,
must i seem so distant?

i am as intimate
as flesh to warmth
as voice to thought;

but there is a son's life
between us.

the mortals 96

and the glowing ticker
counts the revolutions around the sun
mounts our evolutions,
faces flickering
conversing across a continuum
of deserts, jungles and ancient cities:
while the pyramids hover still
with their own sense of scale,
and the postcards in the letterbox
send proximity across distances.
and still, and still
flesh segregates flesh
and hearts
wriggle as fish in sunken mesh
as food for fishermen
or prey to sharks,
their eyes translucent with fear
in the Dark Ocean.
and miners claw for diamonds,
stars in the coal sky
as silicosis breeds itself.
breeds itself in breathing
of whispered lives that
dream and die

and our gesturing hands
find their mother
in silence,
our words having left
our tongues,
hungry for voices,
our mouths,
hollow of meaning.
for as mortals
we know our choices
are only
many little acts of cowardice.

quantum communion   96

enter.
desirable insect.
plunge.
and beg intimacy with my blood.
for you it is red,
viscous vermilion,
to feed your progeny million.
and even as you pierce my skin
your delicateness
declares your destruction as sin.
>   with my extended hand
>   i could but want and
>   desolate your mindless
>   sense of isolation.

taste.
not sugar but
salt.
the ocean that sustains you.
for you are its child,
a subtle surge,
that will rise and then submerge.
and only in that cold fathom
will you find me
as the space within the atom.
within your extended hand
>   that molecular web
>   could you not but know
>   i was always within your grasp.

think.
my wingless angel.
fly.
and join my nervine reverie.
for you are the phrase,
articulation,
my thought in personification.
my most basic element
i need you
both cruel and clement.

>   and now i close my hand.
>   dream and creation
>   of the same grip.
>   a figment of god's imagination.

dispel 96

and i cannot ----------------------------------dispel you
as i do the air from my lungs
for there is always the need
to breathe
that next breath.

and you will FILL me again.

and you do not
             d
                e
                   s
                     c
                       e
                     n
                         d
as a cooling mist
                       d
                     n
                  e
                c
              s
            a
     but,
warm and dancing
in the sun:
such beautifully   alien   refraction

but ascend
to regions of the sky
where even the mind
has no foot
     hold.

you are   i l l u s o r y

in your closeness.

and it was you who taught me to breathe
                    without oxygen;
          who taught me that memory
              has its own futility;

and to love

                    at a distance.

metaphysical butterfly   96

and i dream as a butterfly
with a flight
which pattern of brilliance
extends beyond the form
i have given myself.

as if my shape
was cut from an intricate lace,
carefully placed,
on the curves
of an elegant body
and when this being is
        still,
                i am i
            butterfly is butterfly

but as motion is all things
this being moves
and the lace folds unto itself---
voids overlap
                i = butterfly
this is how i dream
and only a single thread of belief
separates it
                from waking

perception   94

railways converging,
scenes emerging,
without the narrow,
portal-view urging.

trees rip their roots and run,
homes,ships, brave billowing,
puckering landscapes revolting,
subservience and fallowing,
the sedentary
turned
revolutionary.

> once railway rhythms begin
> once there are windows to look without
> from within.

serpentine, safe sailing,
through storms, all impaling,
those without safe roots,
on perceptual railing.

iron womb clicks affection,
compartment,cell enclosing,
glass, invisible imposing,
captive,view without you,
the protection
breeds
direction.

> fare paid,the rhythm commences
> fair, each window a time without,
> until tenses
> able to see a framed dream
> in continuity.

blackhole 94

i am centered
as a star collapsing
retreating within onto myself
'til i am no more than a pill-
bug
on the highway.
and within explosion
i am relapsing
to the despair
that only a vacuum creates
positive is negative
light, dust and voice
only fulfill my consumption
but no more fill me
than breathing
does my mind.

never is a place
it is where the stars are not
it is without you.

water 94

through these bonds
my hands will work
i am the molecular chaos
that swells within dams
dearching covalent weakness
of granite oppression.
still, i am stronger,
for my life gift
can turn swiftly to death.
for i cannot be held,
only channeled
for i am a woman.
for i am water

i stand before you 94

i stand before you
a secret afraid to be told
fearing, losing my mystery
as your every breath
ripples this body
dissolving
what i thought so solid,
so immutable

a mortal
fearing more than death:
that you may dissipate,
phantom in my fingers,
that you may crystallize
every liquid hope
to shatter them.

yet cringing
that you,groping blind
in a strange terrain
will be lost
in the darkness,
the seat of my emotion,
a nothing
that may overcome
and devour you
though i try to hold it choked.

i stand before you.
fearing you, fearing me.
wondering
which fear is real.

mule 94

i am the mule.
i am not the purpose ,
but the means:
born for bearing loads,
my stoop is nothing
to my burden.
saint,murderer, or child,
i know them not
from the pressure
on my back,
and they know me not
from their own feet:
gazing to purple horizons
than to the ugly beast
that carries them,
that marries them,
to their destiny.
i am the caretaker
of histories
and prodding heels
hold no impetus for me.
i do not refuse to move.
i simply refuse to run.

the hand 97

your skin
was a drapery
your ancestry
had lain upon you.
contortionist,
you shaped
that tissue
to your
inhabitation;
stretching the
commercial package
sold to you.
explosion from
within that
seeks and seeps
relief
in the intensity
of your eyes.
one
had only
to look at them
to acknowledge
the hand
within
the glove.

the lover   94

strange yearning
yawning,
my heart , your face.
i am awakened
from dreams
so undesirable
that reality is the sum
of my granted wishes.

every room i searched
desperately,
unceasingly,
for my lover,
face with familiar eyes
entities that have a
privileged seat
in every thought,
every corpuscle,
of all the reality
i will ever need.

door,
dear,
open.
so that i may learn to open
i have
a labyrinth
of memories,rooms
without occupants;
doors locked.

each room
i searched for my lover.
if only i had awakened,
opened a door,
i would have found you
there.

the nocturnals 95

and in the glades
of rhythm and baritone. . .
i sat among gyrating tribunals
of the nocturnals:
to whom the stars
are sun enough,
and the night
is less a void,
and more a deep brew. . .
that is savored
with every sense
as descending silk of incense
pouring around gesticulation
of hands that speak
when the voice fails.

to sing before the nocturne
here philosophy is
too obscure to be owned;
but is an orphan
fat from charitable hands.
and bodies tightly taken
but slipping as a stream,
names, the sole separation,
only names.

so here;
a glass.
and fill it to the brim
with seraphim,
for i have ingested
the intoxicating darkness;
for even lucifer
was once an angel.

the tear   92

i knew you were going to cry.
    your lower lip became
        a vibration upon a lake
           whose pale pallor
               seemed so calm
                  and serene.
  the eyes that bore into me
      received a glassy depth
         only seen from the edge of sanity
        and though reaching out for safety
          they drew in.
  then,the features arranged themselves
      as if to a song
        so maddening,
          so sudden
            in its vibrations
  it was a common knowledge on the surface
     that these perplexed
     complex arrangements
  must brace themselves for the
     final deafening note
         of reality.

yes, i knew you were going to cry.
  then came the startling anticlimax:
    from one churning orb
    upon that placid cheek
      fell
      a
     single
     drop.

a protest so small and
weightless in actuality
that its futility became its power
as if that shiny bead,
that trembling glass
could reflect the hell
it came from,
and pray for a heaven
Where it could be wiped dry into
an oblivion
and touch perfection.

so ,there you sat:
a lunatic
because of knowledge
a tear
out of desperation
searching for the power of hopelessness
in your presence
and Waiting
shivering
and
shimmering
for your moment of perfection
in
chaos
and
warm
nothingness.

false trees 91

false trees.
born from wombs, hard and geometric,
carried on the gentle hand of wind,
nurtured by the soil, cere's black,cool servant,
called forth by the sun's coaxing and rain's whispers.
destinies of bloom halted by interposition:
by a winter gale or morning frost?
gnarled and twisted , they grew.
looking warm but never loving.
graceful but ever ominous
getting larger
but
never growing.
false trees.

kiss 94

subtle fingers
enmeshed among
the skein tangles
of a morning, a lover's
hair.
whispers,
breath of feline warmth
with the resonance
of falling rain
on petal skin.

words
punctuated

by
a touch
a gaze
and
a kiss.

april winter 95

to make a woman
take the bone
and wrap it with tension
of wire and bandage,
that is pain.
build a bonfire
beneath the damp canopy
of a rainforest
and with an inquisition
of abandoned
undiscovered species
smother it
with a martyr's embrace.

i feel like livingtonight.
i feel like dying tonight.

it rains only enough
to prove how dry is the sand
how dry is my thirst
and the night
exists to contrast
the lightbulb
dimming
spinning
after frantic fingers at flesh
have ceased to struggle.
midnight has at least the moon
and as winter in april.

i have forgotten to grow.

and rain . . . 96

and rain
will wash away all.
tears simply
invite more tears,
but a summer storm
still dispels--------an oppressive heat
                         lifts
       the
           burden
of gravity
from clumsy skin.
and every thought
obtains a glassy translucence
so that every

                    d
                   r
                    o
                     p

of sensation
will reverberate
on the very shores of awareness.
Waterjoiningwater
the ambiguity
      of sky and ocean
ceases to disturb me
although   elusive
      to the GRIP of rationality
embracing all
by d i s s o l v i n g   all
a medium
for all that words destroy.
so,
without   my voice
without   my tears
i wish to sing like thunder.
blossom like lightning,
and rain.

newborn   96

and every morning
i wake as newborn
wriggling
covered still
with the warm residue
of dreams that hover
in my unique possibilities
like fading wisps of clouds.
and my skin shivers
and my eyes hurt to open,
cemented.
for i still hold the ardor,the radiance
                    of sleep
        for i still live there;
            Where conception
                and
                 exertion,
                mind
                and
                matter,
        equally distort the landscape.
            and the morning does not yet
            rape my silence,
            the salience
            of subject and object,
                for i still live there,
where a motion cannot be divorced from its dynamic,
            an origin from its devastation.
            for i still live in
                potentially alternative states
                        of relativity.

amnesiac 96

and this is not my fragile body;
i have glossed over
the vulnerability
that is venerable
within this presence,
Within this cathedral of superb grandeur.
and my tenets,meditations and musings,
my priests,
have decided to augment
their honors
as heirs of eternity,
as heirs of my every aspiration,
to avoid slaughter
in the amnesis
of my elysian fields.
but protect me with your hands;
this final excitatory neuron,
this papyrus is broken.
and in my memory
the confusion, corruption of names
will be punished according
to my
ceremonies of libation
with which i satiate myself
upon
the places of my habitation,
the places of my arbitrary navigation.
but, within this oceanic amnesia,
i shall not be shipwrecked.
for i am a denizen of the moment,
and a transient within eternity.

purlieus 97

i am quiet
and i am convinced of the night.
even on crystalline shores,
the sun caresses the skins
of its suckling creatures,
i am certain of the distance
beyond my fingers.
and no lover's features
could provoke more
sanguinity and incredulity
in granting even a furtive glance to me.

and i am sure that it
knows
i am here,

resolute that it is not empty
with its expanse of stars.

and it is only the will
of this body to breathe,
shivering
burrowing
its brittle fingers
into the soil,
that espouses me to earth.
for the flesh sometimes fears
what the mind worships.
and what the mind worships
is nothing within logical elegance.

closely 96

and there were times
i saw you;
refracted.
sunlight on rain.
and no further than our reciprocal
panoramic mindscapes
did our experiences exceed.
as
fractals
taught us infinity
blackholes
demanded our humility,
and
our wisdom spoke exclusively
of the extent of our unknowing.
and
the stars gave us both
expectation and disconsolation
in their distance.

and we affix as fools
to frozen earth;
to frozen theories of you.

and there were times
i heard you;
rhythmic.
sounds sweet and exotic.
and within our mutual
mellifluous minstrelsy
our utterances could surpass.
as
sonatas
compelled our vociferation,
psalms
sired our enunciations,

and
our eloquence expounded only
our capacity for inarticulation.
and
whispers incite
consonance and dissonance
in their elusiveness

and we cling as secrets
to these cryptic clues
to an unactualized actuality

but
only in a rare bliss
did i ever
witness you.
reflected.
in that silent moment.
as the snow fell soundless
yet obvious.as the ocean was born
yet eternal.
as i closed
my eyes
and regained my sight.
i felt you.

closely as desired.

innocent intoxication   97

would i travel so gladly
if i knew where you stood?
would i venture so senselessly
the fathoms of my wine glass
to find it empty?
but
can i drink so deeply
to fill myself with
an intoxication
so sensing
and
incensing
as a gentle gesture
of attention.
the smile savoring
the silent salience.
and
in such curious depths
i hear
your warm words
at the window;

you slip in like the hour,
holding forever in a cup,
to indulgently devour.

and
your voice
luminous echoes
that liquidate,
that reverberate;
conducting electricity,
conducting a symphony,
making my flesh,
this cellular apparition,
a sporadically gyrating mass
of dancers.

how can you have
such inexpressible ease?

you walk the line
between
innocence and realization,
as a child, humming,
savoring the nectar-filled
ecstasy of a
just-peeled orange.
the pleasure of tasting.
the simple act of being;
unconditionally.

so why do a find it strange
that such
subtle, sensuous serenity
can seduce me?

bats' deity   97

and in the caves,
the prophet spoke
of the face of god,
to the bats,
converts of their own
faceless philosophy.

when lips formed
"mercy"
their leather wings
caught a breath
of sanctuary.
and each weeping scripture
echoed but did not illuminate
their sightless cities
of thought.
and with his screams
"believe!believe!"
the screech of their voices
threw
back, back
from the craggy walls
the sounding face
of the bats'deity.

surface as resonance.
texture as assonance.
words become as bricks.
poetry becomes a cathedral.
and in the empty spaces,
a new species of belief.

and had we not eyes
would god have a face?

or
would it be
some echo
immaculate
in its purest of tones . . .
a silence
stubborn and mysterious
in its austerity blessed
in its proximity
 or
impossible
in its distance?

or
a lucious eloquence
in the most sublime
of articulations.

but,
we as prophets preach
the perfection
of our apparent parables,
making prodigal
all realities
alien to our perception.

but,
a god
with arms,
with legs---
with a face----
is just as fictitious,
as a bat's deity.

34

lying in wait
with head back among the reeds,
aphotic currents tug
as fingers to flesh, as vacuum.
immobile, my legs dangle
as a dance before disaster.
i thought i had control.
i thought the water
could not withstand my eloquence,
nor the earth, my gravity,

in the dark caverns
there lies,
buried, the fertility venus.

she conceived us as flower---- as star;
but man redreamt us-------- as temptress.

and upon those fatal dreams aflight,
millennia of slipping feet in sand,
in a reality of pure polarity,
we find the nurture or nourishment
reduced to the senseless,
to weakness,
in the paradigm of antagonism.

and the ocean has become contaminated,
and the sky has become desecrated,
and the star is yet one more domain.
give her one reason to believe you,
and she will grow
give her one justification,
and she may originate
this wondrous destiny.
give her just one purpose
in loving you.

let this be the beginning of eternity.

but it is not the venus voice
we hear.
to the martyr's soliloquy
the false darwinians
dance. rant.
as mad scapegoats mute
with the cannonade of arrogance,
drunk with limited philosophy,
as beggars in the streets of elysium.

and still she sits,
her eyes,the patient shape of infinity

she received us as child---as dream,
but man's tools reduced us---to seducers.

and voices raised as trumpets,
whimper and wheeze,
their wings ripped by the spires
of delusion;when only a simple silence,
a listening ear,
can rouse the sleeping
in the city of the awakened.

and respect has become intimidation,
and dream has become rationalization,
and power's single dimesion is pain.
place in her soil a seed,
and you will grow.
place in her hands one question,
and you will see it is an answer.
place in her trust your wonder,
and you will love her.

let this be the beginning of eternity.

the moment 97

a gentle tempest,
leaves orange,
leaves me

in sky blue-violet
and rain electric.

i felt inviolate.
shivers subtle
within my skin,
fingers reaching out
from within.

everything whispered
as the leafed ground
announced my arrival.

it felt like
the awkward naked
moment
before intimacy;
knowing
like a rapid pulse in the neck.
darkness
had its own illumination.
blue
as an unending eye,
speaking
as a rambling thought,
thunder
as a distant falling foot.

the moment
was coming for me.

hermit 97

raw wound
your heart
your features
did not disturb themselves.

pain
but
not a quiver,
not a shiver,
not a tremble
on your lips.

regulating your breathing
masterfully
as one who has had practice
in such emotions.

eyes fierce,
defying intrusive
glances,
lances
into the sea that swallowed
you.
confusing
any attempt
at interpretation.

silence
your entombed sphinx lips
sliced,severed
all connection,
as some lone defiant tree
pulling back its roots.

accidental epiphany,
your furrowed brow
and
granted a level of unseen
depth to your face
as you eclipsed yourself;
always secluding to the far
table
preoccupied with your own
complexity.

a knot
in the undoing
perfecting your gestures.
a nomad;
among the dramas around
you.

the tongues
you speak
have softened,
your eyes
have hardened
and in the explosion
you are a dissipation;

a shadow
casting your world in
anonymity,
a hermit
reluctant in your
closeted synchronicity.

chance creature   97

your lips pulled back a smile,
your eyes reclaimed their rightful privacy
as
your hand gently rediscovered the contours
of your own profile.

could you be any more aware of yourself?
could you be any less aware of yourself?

as if in some
walking,
waking,
transcendence you focused yourself within
your exclusive, surreptitious imagery.
where words would walk
carelessly crushing
any tender subtlety,
fragile phenomenon,
leaving doubt and confusion
as scattered debris
in their wake.
awake.

your hands curled against your chest.
your shoulders held only by inherent structure
and
your senses cloistered any unprotected
vulnerability.

could i know you any more?
could i know you any less?

as slipping fingers
clenching,
clutching,
you dropped below my consciousness
losing yourself to your private alphabet.
somehow you sang,
deliberate and dwelling,
eyes, caverns swelling,
hands compelling,you pulled me down,
in a secret night,
tonight.
two vulnerabilities
within
excruciatingly beautiful
proximity.

40

dreamt i   97

dreamt i was christ
ready to be a martyr
in a room
of shelves,
of kindling,
then
dreamt i was kindling
ready to be burned.

dreamt i was christ
kneeling
some self -sacrificial,
some self-superficial
lamb,
clear jewel of a head
in a room of costumes
then
the disguises painted me.

dreamt i was christ
waiting to be crucified,
my disciples,
a scream of drunkards;
my audience,
a little girl
staring at the sky
staring at a burning building

and then

dreamt i was her
running from men
because she had
become a woman
(a crime punishable
by cruelty
in most states (of mind))
then running through
a confusion of doors
where one door must close
for one to open.
(a habit that usually
arranges a circle)

then

dreamt i was 50
(it was my birthday)
telling a little girl
that i
dreamt i was christ.

fragility 97

what fragility
held me to this silence?

unwilling to shatter
the continuous glass of
your abstraction,
my thought,
aching limbs,
swaying in oceans of reverie.
as i trudged and stumbled
into speech,
the immediate and the logical,
statues of some strange
spring carnival passed
breathing the most
torn whisper.

and you sat, eyes closed
with the peace
of a sitting buddha;
with the awareness
of a yet disrupted wind,
of a yet delusioned child

i knew you
by your hands;
by the enigmatic mountain
range
that was your knuckles,
by the flitting moth-like motion
of your fingers.

and as i spoke,
your eyes rose
slowly,
unveiling jewel blue,
unending river askew
with its own reflection.
welcoming me
with a smile,
creeping back your face,
rain on a window
streaking across my mind;
a window without light.

cradled
comfortably
in your own arms
as i
in your presence.

she told me 97

her deep-chocolate,
cinnamon-speckled face,
obsidian eyes,
worn suede lips;
they told me.

of two daughters
tall, gangly
and gregarious,
who laughed at her
in the shower.

of mother and daughter,
a war,
cold with separation,
until a stroke
granted a truce
in death.

of brother and sister,
who she,
always mother
at 12.

of a baby
she carried in
the half existent womb
the doctor had left her.

of a man,
of a marriage
she was not ready for.
"maybe when i'm 30."

of a cancer,
of the sparse growth
of hair
under a black scarf.

of hips that had grown.
of a father who had not.

through her perfect smile
that still managed to inhabit
that face;

she told me.

insomnia 97

music,
ending of a 3 A.M. movie.
too afraid to sleep-
not fear of the dark-
but
of eyes closing
for the last time.
because
the empty echo
of electric humming streets
        is not restrained
by the window.
realizing your own pulse
as your cigarettes run low
smoking them
        to give accent to the void.
as your throat
        itches like the flu.
lives flickering on a screen,
mute,in low volume
and
they seem
        forgotten.
dust on tables,
dirty glasses,
        half hidden wrinkles in flesh,
as their glow illuminates
a god's face.
performing
until a finger upon a button,
until the universe,
collapses
into a single spark
that fades
leaving a memory
        on the retina
as morning diffuses
        the night
with blessed distraction.

the quietening 97

it comes a 3 A.M.
it comes too late.
it comes too early.

it is not
a decaying corpse
that eventually
explodes,
but
something living
twitching
refusing to die.

it is not a gash
in flesh
from serrated edge,
but a half-healed
aching just within
the skin.

it is the warmth
against lungs
after drinking coffee
with frostbitten hands.

it is despair and hope.

it is the sound
between sighs;
flutter of lash
of the descending eye.

it is internal agreement
with disagreeing truth.

it is the gentle stroke
of a thumb
across fingers of a barely
clenched hand
in good-bye.

it is the snow falling.

it is the moistening of a lip
before a kiss.

it is headlights
reflecting back from
a wild eye.

it is the time
between glances.

it is a glance
without time.

it is the quietening

and it is anything
but quiet.

bradbury's pedestrian 98

silent
you gasped
a fish for breath,
abyss eyes
glazed
with self-epiphany,
with awed glimpse
at your place
within infinity.

mouth slacked
you gazed
through a stray
windswept hair.
you arms
cradling,
sustaining yourself
with your own touch.

runaway
clutching your coat;
two small fists
clenched purple
in icy air-
teeth-biting-lip,
mute of angry silence.

head turned
to escape
a memory
fast approaching
as a car collision.

eyes wincing
to the sound
of broken glass,
of twisted metal,
resounding
in your
grinding teeth.

my arms
in wanting-
to embrace,
to feed
an appetite
starved, a lifetime
you fed one meal,
a mouse nibbling.

what it was?
it was birth-induced
alienation
without
explanation.
so much the color
of your eyes
that i never-
until now-
saw it look into me.

you,
bradbury's pedestrian.

even now 98

and even now
i can imagine
the wide flat fingertips
of your philosopher's hands
gently warming
and defining
the contour of my arm,
the curve of my neck,
as you push back the strands
of my hair,
as you pull back the curtain
of my
strategically distracted
attention
a tension
that in chilling
burns.

and
even now
i cannot imagine
a voice
as acquaintance
speaking my name
as baptism
as blessing
the eye that smiled
gazing
as a perfect tone
to the ear
with honesty
that makes a liar
of me.

though ,even now,
i see you
wrinkle under the eye
i turned from
sun-smile eclipse
by feigned demure
allure
of your laughter.

so that it is
only now
a memory
of a hand brushed
in passing
that i should
have clasped.

paper doll 98

paper doll.
you cut me out of context
just to make conversation.

and i smile
to keep the child
behind your proper
folded hands
from ripping me
as i ,
as you
fold me
into your purse.

and as a child
you babble with a toy;
pretending to speak to it,
pretending to listen.

you say
honesty
is why they hate you.
you say
my façade
is why they love me.

but there is no polite
way to say
you think me
a liar.

do not give
too many
dimensions
to your
paper doll.

you dress me
in whatever suits
your needful beliefs.

i was your
whipping bitch.
i was your
counselor
i am your
trophy
and your
custom made
inquisitor.

i am
your paper doll.

annunciation 98

i will be no mona lisa.
i will be no venus.
my eyes will never
            have verses.

i will be no juliet.
he will be no romeo.
such deaths for love
            have no purpose.
such worship
            has no substance.

i will be no helen.
not your justification
            for escalation.

i will be no mary.
                        not your purification
                        nor deification.

i will have no pygmalion.
                        you did not sculpt me
                                    nor bring me life.

i will not be eve.
you will not hold me liable
to a guilt deniable.

not your altarpiece.
not your centerpiece.

i will not negate
my meaning
to be your talisman.

delphine '98

eyes of a delphine oracle I know what will happen next but only because it has happened before. the volcanic ash has preserved the footprints of those who have run before us, from the fire, a judgment to the unnamed and to the cataclysmic even for the elaborate folds of the smart monkeys brain. "why?" the shortest word to start the longest of journeys. oh, no, the second shortest

shortest

i

initiate 98

and your arms
said my name
the intertwining threads
of an incantation.

lips rounding
every syllable ,
some echo
in an empty alley;
some rapidly rolling
thunder
over a crimson desert.

as if your voice
could conjure me
in my every
configuration

and your eyes,
silver shark
serenely slicing
the secrecy
of my ocean.

a voice
quiet and distant
a primordial darkness
reaching for me
an undulation
in the membrane
that so
rupturably
enveloped me.

as my skin
a wolf reposed in
quiet intensity;

my staring
and your smiling

as some apologizing child,
your thick fingered hands
approach,
a creeping lucid eyed nocturnal
testing the fragile underbrush
the curve
behind my ear.
searching
the ivy of my hair
as if to see my thought
elusive helix serpent
as if to know
what occupied my eye
as to immobilize
my lips
in half-spoken word.
waiting
for me
to resurrect
an ancient alphabet
from the dust
upon the moistening
of my tongue.

and my folded hands
dared not betray
your worship
with the gropings
of an initiate.

dream - thanksgiving 1998

it was the end,
or so you said,
and we were
alone
in this last moment.
outside the walls,
you told me
of masses of panicked
bodies

looting store windows
grasping
for the icons
they never let
themselves have.
only in the end
do we let ourselves.

as you stripped
off your clothing,
such ease
in the act,
such cold
seductioon,
you invited me
to swim.

laughing
at my modesty
irrelevant
as if
at world's end
my heart should
feel less fear,
my skin
should shiver
less
in the cold air.

the water
it glowed
crystal blue.

and i only
stepped
toward the door
and asked you
why it was locked,
i needed proof
it was the end.

so that
i may let myself.
and outside-
streets of calm
leading children
in the average hours
of an average day
it was not the end.

i stood before
a window,
fingertips clutching
the soft skin
a bare-assed black
infant in my arms,
someone else's
abandoned child,
someone else's
inconvenience.

i hadn't pulled it
from the end.
it hung listless,
i clutched it,
as if i could stop it
from ending.

52

frostbitten angels 99

angel-
estranged gargoyle
of beauteous curvature,
of hollow torture
within windless perfection.

a touch of numbness.
a fruit without sugar.

a dark cloak
within me.
shadow casting light
upon the painting
without pores
to cry,
a body that
cannot scream.

but the ocean sings.

please
stop walking above me.
stop leaving footprints
within the sand
of memory
my foam fingertip
will wash
the sublime gaze
you extract
with distance

i will flesh our
the projection
ache within
small of back,
swelling of eye,
lend depth
to a flattened film
that frailty burns
with my breath.

and who knows more
than an outsider,
who feels more
than a distant
spinning planet
who hungers
more than
the sightless singularity -
never fed
but consumes
the light of suns.

my skin
will be my death
my bones
will make me cripple.
my eyes-blind.
but i know more
in my longing,
within my unknowing
than
frostbitten angels.

gollum 98

gollum   -and more resentful
my anger
the silt-   and sleep is broken.
   and i rise
my skin,   deliberating movement
grit pebbled mud-   with mechanisms
the texture   of an epileptic
of my hair   my limbs take
slinking,   unintentional victims
sinking,   with their
in black congealed   conditioned flailing.
sanctuary
silent depth   enveloped,
of swamp.   i am silence.
   blind,
within sleep   i am darkness.
my fingers   curled,
sculpted   i am vulnerability.
the dark sockets   minstuned string
of my eyes.   of nerve,
   veins of nightmare,
and still my stare   i am pain.
is dull   primordial
with the caul   in unending need.
of unforgiven
memory.   labrynthed
   in a crevis
   of thought,
and with fingernail,   given a hollow life.
carved
a name   forgive me.
an abomination-   i am a demon
a fire   trying to be a gargoyle;
upon the ocean   in walking,
an incantation   a spirit
in pronounciation,   within dermal layers
a word   some driftwood
shaping dust   too brittle to embrace
against an opal moon

wind in pursuit   in my fugue
of stillness.   i am trying
in sleep,   to protect memory.
i have only grown
teeth,claws

54

primal 98

"not all of us
lack kindness."
breathless gust,
warm at my neck.

you held my shoulders,
looked into my eyes.

so, strange messiah,
glimpse
into my most inner need.

i
resisted and begged,
lame creature
so commonly ravaged,
fear
that even the most
benevolent predator
might kill me.

my body,
pasty imperfection,
surrounded
by the
immaculate circle
of your large shoulders
tanned arms.

you were sky-
hovering in expanse,
gentle in subtlety

you had no need
to exaggerate
your power.

you patiently
stroked the skin,
between
rib and waist-

going no further-
slowly
weaning me
from cruelty

i was silent.
you said
you'd never hurt me.

i looked away,
trying to
comprehend
the sun at night

leave me numb.
i am the mermaid
without a tail.
i cannot return
to the ocean.

i will become foam,
dissolving
upon your skin.

the price for feet.

and i dissociate
in direct proportion
to the proximity of skin.

the ache
of your body.
and my closed eyes.

i drank its intensity.

not the innocence
of children
but the sensual
honesty
of primal infants.

paintings 99

what shall i name
what i have painted.
some beings faces
are their names
their curves,shadows
too indescribable,
too toxic,
to twist a tongue upon.

as irresponsible parent,
geneticist in pigment,
my mutations
infest the walls
in my sleeping.
allowed
to witness
the daily faulterings
of creator
to see god
sneeze and cry.

my intimacies
have forgotten
flesh within
a less relentless skin,
caressing canvases,
always closer
to my bed
than you.

and my fingers, cold
i run then under
warm water
so the joints move
so i can paint;
arching ancient scribe.

and their mouths
are words

i promised
i would say, someday
their eyes
the quietly observing child
that one day
speaks
in alien minds
the secrets that
silence
has given them

do they pity
the fleshed out figment
for being
a midwife of illusion,
for not
making drunken love
upon the floor.

vampiric children
cold from my fingers.

i keep them
with me
some left unfinished,
their wisdom
too precocious
for human
psyche.

and some
i sleep with
a finger stroking
a delicate line
unspoken
degree of perfect.

rather be unspoken
of how much
of me
they have taken.

amphora 99

have i lost
amphora?
her echo
the surrounding
backward
curvature of time
is more wind
than whisper,
excavated
from desert sands
more resonant
than blackness of sky.

but my skin
an unfired
once hardened
clay jar,
now moistening
collaspes into its hollow.
no pain,
just a stare
into my own
brittle concavity.

through me,
she spills her
contents upon
the thirsty land.

blood,
dark soil
that flowed up
through tree
her veins
upon the sky.

milk
the creatures
suckle upon
river and rain
lips to swollen breast.

skin
the canopies of forest
entangling,
conspiring
to conceal
her small hands
with the expanse
of their palm.

and with fingers
like mine,
she plucked the berry
and
dug the root.

and lips
older than mine
tasted toxin and cure,
spoke tradition.

but it became
his medicine,
his lesson.

and her face
the first
the child learned.

but he pronounced
himself god.

and in the pages
before the book,
the ink faded.
and in the earth
before the world,
she was buried.
and in the story
before HIStory,
a brittle scroll,
a dried placenta.

she had given birth
to an ungrateful son.

jack 99

i never realized
how handsome he was-

-just thought
the photograph
a momentary sobriety,
a paper mid-flutter
puddle stained
by rain,
by her
merciless fingertips.

but handsome?

maybe it was
before rivers
carved canyons
around his eyes,
islands
dark mossed
with primal jungle
upon a sea,
deaths milk;
a skin, a granite
that the
nail scratching wind
reduced to talc.

evidence
that beauty
could not
resist,desist
the claws
dragging wildly
from eye to mouth,
a mad cat.

did wine
make his genius
or
genius make his wine
whine-
dark rasp whimper
poking-ribbed stray
nostrils flared
upon the scent
of his own mortality.

did he really know
that pain as i do?
of being
a blood -bone -tissue mirror
of every fingertip,
every voice unspoken,
whispers,
their still mouths open
in awe of the void
before them-
that is my present-
the pain of mannequins
in a tornado-

his face now
a lunatic
caught in the act
of being sane,
a human,
caught bleeding
memories
through his eyes,
drinking them
to blur
the photograph.

(for Kerouac)

58

the bell 99

the sound of the bell
was distorted
by the halo of wind
off my back
as i ran away.

until the bell was. silence

in proximity it sang,
consuming the ear
as zealous teeth
consumes the mind
as thoughtless faith.

it leaves no room
for other sounds.

and i ran
when i was eight
the bell had demanded
deafness,
a mute ear
in those who listen
too closely,
too long.

its choruses louder
to cover a scream
a millenium-and more
of hate;
decreeing
that some cover
their ears,undeserving
of its tone.

i quietly turned away

so young
and even
knew bells could lie.

at weddings,
a promise of fidelity,

love-within obedience
silent
about the bruise.

at baptisms,
a promise of safety
under a wing

the terrorist threat
of original sin
in its echo.

at funerals
mourning,
mocking
the pain
of living and loss.

it pretended it knew.

but i found something
more holy in heathens
devils,
know more of humanity;
drunks,
more of sobriety;
prostitutes,
more of purity,
and killers,
more of life's fragility.

my education
was the full flesh
of these shadows
that light refuses
as little more
than an effect
of its own brilliance,

as the bell
regarded silence
as empty
with its absence.

now the bell
is more hushed
as i pass.

i do not have to run,
it knows not to pursue
i know its lies,
it only whispers
to tempt me back.

lead me not
into temptation.

i turn away.

i accept no promise of love
with half acceptances.

the enveloped 99

the light
molested your features;
an unwelcome illumination.

you would prefer
to remain hidden,
a mass of flesh
surrounded
by the smoke
of the cigarette
that absolved
you from any
obligation
to converse.

but even so,
your skin reflected
light
in a socially desirable manner;
satin cut
to a novel
invented style.

laughs surrounding
too drunken
to block your ears to

(theirs being some
desperate claim
of happiness)

writing themselves
upon you.

but the imperfect voices
asserted themselves,

you wondered
what braid held such
creatures bound
and why that knot
excluded you.

only a wisp of thread
occasionally brushed
your skin,
a misplaced whisper
displacing your thought.
you searched their faces
sporadically
hoping
that a drunkenness
would carry in its,
tunneling haze,
an insight
you could feed upon
in private,

but gently
released your glass
as if placing
aside
some pre-decided worry.

last days   99

the wind,
the concrete runn,ng
ripples streaming,
cosmic lightning
screaming,
clouds rasping,
as time elapsing,
mind relapsing
to primordial desperation.
a child jaw clasping
time,
creature of magnitude
passing,
its movement evident
only in its pull upon
the tide.

and the sea
grips the shore
to hold itself to earth

but the
Dark Ocean
dilates and blossoms
much more slowly.
its glowing creatures

eyes
thin,shimmer plates
full,black,pearl

to dine upon the void
(only stars know the
abyss as they do)
their fins
brush and tickle
our desires
scuttling,
huddling,
needful,many fingered
urchins upon the floor;
maneuvering
within gelatinous rhythms
numb to the pull
of an unseen celestial
that pulls upon the
unwise or unrooted
its misty
barely-breath
bending the sky
at even this distance.

and the wind
an invasive, erotic hand,
no!-

and the rain
knows
my hair
as only my hands do.

and the ocean
the angry pulse
behind my smile.

awaken 99

and i am
back from the dream,
remembering another,
blood ache murmur
broken blood vessel
within my breast.

i have grown
accustomed
to its beak in me,
the seed
it tries to feed me.

crow mother
i sit with my mouth open,
in awe - not hunger
i've been fed too much
more than i can hope
already
to digest.

ruminate this soft,pasty
comprehension
before i enter
another darkness.

the dawn of predawn
upon me
i wonder if birds
are just voices,
just means by which
the sky sings.

and my sleep-drugged
brain
knows more,
remembers more,
than it will
when days sun
awes these graceful,
slithering nocturnal shadows
into their holes.

the sun shines
in fear.
for the night
is surrounding
and not afraid
to allow minds
in the void between stars
under barely smooth
back of,
black of
a crow's wing.

silence 99

and what of this silence?
am i a bubble
unable to support
its pressure
upon my fragile surface.

it forces,
as if underwater,
my thoughts
back upon my ears.

a voyeur
without interest,
without perverse
curiosity,
my nakedness
does not intrigue it.

my skin
only a curve
resounding
its nonexistent echo.

it needs me

no more than the air
needs my lungs
to breathe it.

only trees need that.
only we need each other.

no more than
the sun needs earth
or the void
its reflection
ender blue iris
upon an infinite
pupil,
dilating to its own darkness.

no more than god
needs us
upon our knees.

these beings
are merely watching
passed the scene.

ocean and mountain
are blasphemous screaming
adolescents
by comparison.

is their wisdom
remembering-or forgetting.

undesiring buddha,
embracing gaia,
handwringing kwan - yin,
vengeful yah-weh.

is its fugue
forgiveness
or
simply knowing
every electron
will remember for it.

silence
is not empty.

it is too full
of our questions.

caffeine dream 99

hour 1

this is not real,
emptying into the
south china sea.
the shorter hair
day-dreamed
consequences of the
rainy season,
an ideogram for
monsoon
fingers with sanctity
of scarlet
trickling from a nail.
christ was a vampire
that fed upon others
in his own bleeding.

he danced
with carnal celts
eyes glazed
to their flesh filled
straw dogs
burning in a solstice night

a dirge of slow oozing
lightning
sang behind the stars,
distant eyes glistening
as predator or parent.
the smile is usually
the same.

hour 2

a white noise that
knows the threshold
of my ears sensitivity.
all the screams,
requests and whispers
that fill it, overflowing
overpowered

by their own
sentimental
PTSD memory

and they have colors for
rhythms
and the colors
of yours is red-
no, the color
of yours is the pink-gray
only summer twilight
knows.

but it makes me red
for makes me bleed
the manner of invasion
how it outlines
and pronounces
the shadow
of the dark trees
to those dark creatures
that dance behind
my consciousness
with changeling dexterity
(morphing rather than moving.)
creatures of
habitual use-
but you drag them
out in full
with your kindness,
your kind.
you are kindred
with your keys
to my back door.
-poking at the wound
the scar remembers
-a leviathan surfacing
-a crow with
its soul burdened
wings alighting.
-a pupil dilating
in the half whisper
of a dark room
of an abandoned
childhood home.

hour 3

and then
pound
upon the door.
a voice conjuring
with its inflections,
infections
the force
of the
meaningless jabber
the gurgle
of the drowning
of the last breath.

but i know what
it is saying,
the largest shadow
an expansive
hemisphere sky
of lie,waiting
its babbling
with rapid instance

the list of my crimes
grime
and the rain hisses
upon the road outside
i stand silent
hopeful its torrent
will melt,dissipate
this gollum.

but is has only
gone silent
with a patience
that graves demonstrate.
i knew that its eyes
glazely gaze upon
the closeness of the door
thoughtlessly
awaiting me.

waking

am i supposed to dance for mussolini?
darkness insensibly surrounding
rain rustling,shuffling my private papers

but it is best to say
nothing of strange dreams.

drink in silence
as if surgery
were in progress
and a gnat squallors
sqeaks like a rusted door
in half-thought
of closing
-it sounds like anemia

the coffee was correct
i will not sleep.

cradle 99

and i can imagine
how earth must feel.
scarred
by her creatures,
children
feeling their way,
nails of such small fingers,
such desperate attention,
clawing into her skin.

she will survive us.
she will not die.
in childbirth
but
has the wisdom
not to push us out
of the cradle.
we rape her.
we already have.

my eyes
close and thank
the abyss
for its distance
that star
is placed far
from our hands.

we shouldn't leave
until we learn.
our fingers should
fall
upon empty darkness
until we know
the full power

of our grasp
the impact
of our touch.

until our hands
are not as needful
as an infants mouth
and god is quiet.

and earth is patient.
the abyss, discipline
within its
gentle expanse.
those eyeless
beings
have more sight
than refracted light.

and we await
the vision
in the window
the demonstration
of power
we borrowed
from the atom.

the veil einstein
lifted.

but before the blast
the shadows whispered.

an insight
with even
more lucidity.

knowing 99

the transfixed
wonder
of a child--
the ability
to hold attention
to the most
unnoticed
of flickers,
an inhabitor of corners
precociously fading
into the wallpaper,
into the peripheral,
casting aside
the heavy garments
of ego,
to quietly observe.

most hearing
the rage
scrambling
between your clenched teeth
think your first instinct
is to scream.

but those thin
hushed lips
seem more to me
trying to manage
a meek smile
as eyes intent
recede when met.

and i smiled
betraying
through deliberately
oblivious calm
that i felt you
--almost smiling.

a priest fixated
upon
a buddha.
an ancient
behind poreless
porcelain skin.

you knew
i knew
you watched.

studying the flutter
of my lips
sculpting cigarette smoke
the curvature
of fingers
in the writing of
of this word.

you even tried to blink
some shutter
to break the stare-
you know as
the first symptom
of obsession;
an ailment
you thought
you had long
lost
the talent for.

but do you
know
that i have
been watching
you
longer.
and i know
my quietest voice
has awakened you.

watcher 99

there are times
i do not recognize you.

      as if your
skin does not
wrap tightly enough
over your form,
over your truest-shape.
so i am left
to discern
distortion
from you.

      and your
eyes pierce.
two beasts
from the wilderness,
their color
sentinels to your secrets.
a vagueness implied
in dimidiating pupil

no aperture
to step through

and why does
your shadow
come visiting
eyes glistening.

quietly listening

watching
in numbing awe
your own reflection
upon my window.

your silence
speaking to my skin
like gentle rain

eyes of your
lost intention
upon me.

and you have
been there
longer than
night,

but somehow
star
is older.

a moon
the mother
you suckle upon,
some alien
singularity
unknowing
of its own
hunger.

some watcher
satiating
itself
upon me.

the dead 99

hair
gorgeous flow glacier
of black ice,
it glimmered
in its stealth.
the jittering quiver of lip
upon my name
its breath.

the dead
they walk with skill
upon the rafters
and say much
with whispers
that out-scream
the disturbed,
now settling, dust.

and they have us
surrounded.

they swell
and they smell
the living.
bloated with infection
they know
sweet sweat
and
unpowdered blood.

and a scratch.
a stroke of finger,
a kiss,
and they have you
blank,martyr-eyed
marley-jawed
perpetual disposition
of awe
that lazarus
probably had;

its parasites
upon the meager resource
of the mortal eye.
expanse of singularity
in such limited dilation
of pupil.

yes, that awe
the dead know
damp cold and misty
that would a finger
reach,misplaced
it would uravel
fingernail splintering
caught upon
thread of tapestry.

peeling back
the bloodied bandages
upon consciousness.

they know
that in some
bubbled off
spawn of time-

our scenes
still play
ourselves.

a murder,
a molestation,
a darkness
repeats
as if anew,

in temporal
unknowing.

they know
we leave ghosts
even as
we live.

leaving eden 99

and i am tired
of watching unnecessary pain.

(eve was simply precocious.)
the fruit was not the poison-
no snow white sleep-
but an awakening
from a womb
we clawed desperately
to crawl back into.

too unwilling-
rather to dream
in floating darkness.
that first Dark Ocean,
that insatiable
one sided intimacy.
rather to grow,
in refusal to leave
to rupture
the mother's womb,

than to breathe
our own breath,

than to live the dreams
nine months
prepared us for.

but we leave--
no mother,
no uterus,
is tolerant enough
for such prolonged denial.

nor should it be.

and within that blaze
that first blinding retinal fire
our minds
manifest the universe
in our own form.

and in her arms.
she is god.

without
ideology or theology.

and
youareher.

her fingers
are your pulse
her voice,
your prayer.
the ever-dilating pupil
of her eye-
the only starlit sky
you need.

and then,
the feet walk,
the coos talk,
and the ears
translate
those previously
translucent streams
of sound,
eyes see
clearly into depth
the subtlety
of here and there.

ofyouareher.

and you walk   away.

and here it goes astray.
i say it was not the fruit,
not even the snake
but
the thundering voice
that pronounced
her wrong--
and us guilty by
reproduction.

it was the pen
that misunderstood
the story.

that forgot the name
of the tree--

knowledge.
it is still astray.

the curse
just because
we learned to walk.

a curse
the child cries-
because there is
no reason to crawl
anymore.

and too many reasons
to run,

but we crawl back
on our knees
for millennium
begging
for entrance
to the womb
that is too small for us now.

and fist chisels
into flesh.

rite of passage
of cain.

and here
it is still astray.

deified defied 99

you're right
this glazed
night consumed
stare betrays
the pulse
that in its
cavernous deposits
forms my claws
and teeth.

i am colder
than the warmth
of my lips
testifies.

but i am
uniquely qualified
for my position.

you are black
expecting
me white.

you cannot
oppose me
for i have not
the naivete
to be absolute.

demons can only
defeat angels
with their
philosophical
underminings
of
immaculate conception.

the mere mortal
takes more convincing.

teeth
dull from overuse
claws
minimal in grip

and
night only so numbing
without stars
demons
only fabrications of fear.
empowered only
by our impotence.

break only the skin
of the bleeding.

but mortals,
dangerous distortions,
have only
silence of moon

and are lunatics.

god answers not
our transmissions
into the void.

peasant farmers starve
in the aristocratic
chess war
of god and devil.

they only know
the barren field.
maddened beyond ideology

as soldiers
abandoning fronts
of crusades
deserters
deserving more.

tufts of angels
feather the mud,
blood of devils
drinks the rivers.

i see only the sky.
i feel only the ocean.

an ancient sense
impartial
staring into each other.
into each others
infinity.

and what truths
are in such a gaze?

and could i
a mortal
reflect in such mirrors.
to realize that light
is the only glass
unbroken.

winds
icy incantations
whispers
of the back throated growl
of perfection.

could i swim out so far
as to break that gaze
so that they
may see me.

or would that
gaze
break me.

spirit walk   99

and i was
shaken from my sleep
by the shuffling
of
an ancestor's
bones,

the earth is dust;
they move.
the earth is dry;
they rise.

a drum of thunder
white blood of light
a liquid pulse of fire
a heart
of many voices
unintelligible
but
articulate
to the ache
within my throat.

i am the rind
of an aged
hand.

not a photograph
as memory
but an embrace,
the coil unwinding
lazarus

and
their voices
are canyons
their song,
a starlit surrounding.

their eyes;
as the desert
they see.

as healing as cactus
a gentle sting
water
upon
an air drowning throat,

they bring the ocean
and the moon
to me.

the desert dances
as a gypsy.

stream of moonlight
upon my eyes.

the wind
an ecstasy
the cloud
a rhythm.

hand dug
into cooler depth of soil.

spirits
that touch
in bleached bone
of wisdom,
of blood.
more than a human hand
brittle
the kindness
that is not swaddling,

but
open sky.

and i am
rivers,
my fingers
search the solace
of my sub-dermal
creatures.

through wildest jungle
the darkest
recognize me.

they know
the patient pounding
of my pulse
and
the cadence
of my breathing.

gray 99

a thought well
meandered,
the ocean
stretches
its horizon,
carnivorous.

a thin
needful strip
of land
barely satiates
its gaping mouth.

a gray abyss
hungrier
than any black
the not quite
predatory
memory
that is the plump
fullness
of every cell.

it wants
what it has given.

its distance beacons
blinking

it seduces
with reflection,
the vain;

with its silence,
the thoughtful.

and at night
the air addicted
creatures
sit at barely secure
proximities
to whisper
secrets to each other.

the ocean sleeps,

an unfathomable
boundary
with its fathoms.

the milk
of the forgotten,

its glisten
the clarity
of yearning,

of the muted
hurtful
throat,

of the voice,
screaming of eye,
still of lip.

a dark thread
bound
and lost in
gray.

quiet desperation 00

psychological loveliness
you believed,somehow
in a world,
an undercurrent
below
this flesh-coin-
rain and sun
one.
and accepted
that maybe-this belief
was just madness.
facing it calmly;
skin as moon
though
your stomach ached
with its implications.

sighing
as a means of breathing
of releasing,
relieving it.

you confessed to me lunacy
private acts and rantings
mystical child associations.
you confessed to me loneliness
conversations with only the
imagined,wished would be there.

you knew
that as crimes
(despite public stoning
by eyes and silence,)
that these were common
and as unenforceable
as jaywalking-
the shortcuts used
to cross quickly
through bitter winds.
the more permissible
were only those
we nodded our heads to
in collective shivers.

but we all know
and
we all thought
we,the only ones
hiding otherwise

we are the
unexplosive terrorists,
killer's with
graveless cellars,
emily dickinsons
with no poems
in the wallpaper,
the janis joplins
that never went
to california.

the christ
to judas,
the judas
to christ

we are without that moment.

masses of history
without
historical significance.

our biographies-
our epitaphs

and the blemishes
wrinkles,cavities, gray hairs,
of our deprivations.

and you felt it
cataloging, filing;
your soul an archive
for those
you could not see die

some merciful care
that
no one be forgotten.

mother 99

i turned
in my sleep
a verse
upon the time
in my ears.
eyelid
shuttered open
a void searching.

and as
fragile child with candle
i wandered
corridors
i wondered
if the world had ended.

would it end
in darkness.
in one premorning,
would we all
be turned
to find
the veil from
the hand
had fallen

and see
a dervish dancing
in sublime blissful bare
entirety.

would we have
that second
to see,
if it ended.

trembling virgins
in consummation
with a more
prenatal knowing
of newborn.

once more
back
into the
oblivious breathless
word
of womb.

as we cradle
upon
the blue planet.

mother's
space-time skin
surrounding;
suckling upon
her silence.
eyes as stars

she looks on
me with patience.

a child
not quite managing
a footstep
clinging to the light
of candle.
that must
extinguish
this flesh.

and as i cry
some pseudo
homi-suicidal
scream,
the ache
a blackhole
dilating in my chest.

she restrains her hand.

she cannot make me live.
though she can keep me
alive.

and anguish denounces
a hermit's resolution,
an anarchist's
gritting teeth.

a warrior's sword
slicing futile blow
into a spirit.

she is merciful
but resolute
with my tantrums.

even as i
pronounce
my lonely
sovereignty.,

she holds me.

dream sometime in 1999
(four hours)

hour 1

a tribal drum chants
an incessant.
pulse of blood,
while a madman rants
to the deep, hollow concavity
of a half-empty-full
translucid green grass
bottle.
and the city conspires
with its invasive
many-fingered
noises.
the world never quite silent.

hour 2

and the poet stands
upon a high school stage
against a burgundy fade
of velvet,
a light within a darkness
of folding chairs.
his voice, an echo
the oxygen resonant
with the adolescence
beneath gray hair.

and how
we admonished him
his words
but words
surround as womb
and we remember
when a heartbeat
was that close.
and blood was wine
pulsing into our navels.

we remember the future
as we once thought,
before our healthy
soul cleansing,
our conversion to reality
safer behind unexpressive
faces.
now we smile and cry
back into the darkness,
the shadow where sometimes
the most fearful
are not grotesque,
but the round-faced
glisten wide-eyed
to which we forget our debt.
a child-left in a car-mom
gone shopping
"promise, i'll be back soon."
and orphaned - we still stare
but a car's winter window
fogging with our awaiting
breath.

and we become fostered
by our adopting delusions.

and they try
with their pleasantries
to hold you rapt-raped
father-brother-husband
kindness
does it exist?
or just a lie

a worm
smiling
to bore into the earth
between my legs.

hour 3

and awakened, squint eyed
i remember a dream
images fugue
of a child
(receding with a tide
upon a dawn-dewed beach)
a star
whose last light
is just now reaching me,
the afterimage ,
the blindness
from searching the sun.

and across
mind-fields
i walked
a green
a crystal
within its moisture
a carpet rolling
obscuring sky
i traveled
never seeing another.

a shack, my house
that in some
past regression
was a
kick -the-can hidaway
a mom's screaming
a dad's indifference
hospice
and a
"come on, let's go
smoke this" privacy.

where lily of the valley
disrupted,erupted
through the floorboards
lit by the sunstrips
of a half meshed roof.

there i found garments-
outfits i never wore
beautiful, foreign
light weight.
as powder,
as dust upon
my skin
as upon these
shelves

but it was all
gray,
faded as deliberately
forgotten memory
with darkened crevices
and
water ruined upholstery
and a 2 channel-fairlygoodreception-
ifyouturnitacertainway-television.

(they way they can be
when you can tolerate static
and fill in the interference
with your own eyes-
an ability that
ceases somehow
when you can afford
an allchannelscomein-and
nowthere'snothingon.)

and i sat upon
a musk hybrid of smoke and rain
scented chair
gazing upon the tube-dead
reflection of the
inactive screen.

hour 4

when through
a similar window
(a worn aperture in a wall.)
a woman-an ancient-
her daily reenactments
of this moment.
the future of my
self deprivation

but even here
i know i am trespassing.
for
even here
my ownership is
never fully recognized.
possession by
itsallihaveand
itdoesfornow-attachment.
a place i could take for my own
for i knew
no one else would have it
(or halve it.)

and it's being invaded
(even as i watch the old woman
set one plate for supper.)
by real-estate salesman

their eyes threaten with police
if i fuss.
and in the distance
i hear a child scream
but my voice
a barker's cry
drowns it

selling it.

the uncarved   00

even with this crowd,

this martini tipped,
sequin equipped,
trite quip,
battling eyes,
slothing smile,
adrenaline driven,
frenzy
of the collective
willfully unconscious
inanely
questioning you.

you seemed
preoccupied
within the sideward
localities of your eyelids
as if contemplating
the previous
night
of lovemaking.

then upon
the calling
of your name
a hand
pulling you from the ocean,
your submersible sense of
the softness of summer air,
your head,
your smile,
curved upward
a devilish flower
feeding upon the sun.

your lips
even-slivered in
quivering
subliminal
inadvertently
acting upon
the motion of
a kiss.

which upon
awareness
of the multitude
of potential eyes.

you quickly
bit down a lip;

some child
caught in
a pleasurable exploratory.

but
you were suckling
upon a star
that pulsated
to the frequency
to the rhythm
of your
distinct
almost
extinct
species heartbeat.

one million years
in void,
it found
a glowing planet
in your
hoped for intelligence

and to the exclusion
of others sounds.

you listened.

even with so many
thoughts,
you had so few words.

i suppose
the taoists
would approve.

mayan amidst   00

rainforest
healer with
a hovering hand
above the heart,
the black river;
this life
that shatters
my ribs
with its needs.

it would swallow me
if it could exist
without me.

your limbs
entangling
about mine
an oozing vine.
whose warmth
is the sultry
star stricken
tarp
of earth
and night.
arms
the tiger's growl
screaches
in the hollows
of
ancient augeries
its depth and distance
more articulate
than my breathless
tight-lidded
epiphany beholden
sighs
could suggest.

we slept
alone
half excavated
from the forest floor

a slumber,
asunder,
our sounds
in each others ears.
our inhalations
and
our heartbeats,
panicked,
at
the eventuality
of separation.

so we slept
buried in a
time banished
place.

that obscurity
cloistered,
a co-conspirator
of our
ecstatic exile.

we needed no sun
no more
than the
millennia-old
medicinals
that
morassed
and meshed
intermingled
and stretched
their mysteries
in moss softened
flesh;
amidst canopy's mist
as our skin
was nocturnal.

our senses
atoned and attuned
to each other,
to the silence.

my hair
enskiened
your shoulder,
as your whisper
my ear.

the sky slightly lifted
crackled, sifted
out the pitch
of your unsaid
words,
which were
as footfalls
fresh upon mile-far
fallen foliage,
snapping some
stealth
encircling.

i felt myself
a moonlit smile,
from torrent
tidal pools
pulled
by the ethereal
gravity
of never-waking.

the signature
of my features
written with
the indecipherable
characters
of a mayan tile.

pieta   00

you collapsed

sprawling
across my lap.

we were a
hysterically giggling
pieta
even as we
were wounds
bleeding.

as if pain
had made us
anemic
and
in this laughter,
in this pool upon
the pavement,
we found the sun
the winter
had forgotten
to provide.

a victorious insanity.
some unnecessary bonds
loosening.

pinned insects
we writhed under
taxonomic terms
imposed upon us
but also
exhausted refugees
conspiring.
our sedition
was our will,
our crime
was our continued breathing.

all this blood
and we laughed,
orphans
not so unhappily
with out parent.

abandoned by our beliefs
we abandoned our need
for them.
for there was no more
damage
for them
to do to us.

we won
by losing every battle,
by refusing to self-martyr,
by refusing gravity,

and any other law.

digging 00

and what of this
small stone in sand
that curiosity
shaped
my fingers around?

what reflection
gleaned
from its
gleam
of obsidian face?

mine,
partially buried.

one
cliffed, chipped
edge to the sun.

and i dig
expecting it small,
unanticipated depths
it coldly crevised.

sifting silt
with simple
casual, causal
strokes

my hands
thought it
within holding

but
still deeper,
still more.

and the earth
was clay
red-stained
as a mold of murder,
obliviating
my fingerprints
with its
resistant
pressure.

i pried and pulled

but earth
she would not give.

demanding
a more tender
archaeology
to not crack
a curve or cleave
of my philosopher's stone.

my fingernails split,
small cuts
widening, deepening,
bleeding a new strata soil
of the pulse
i must recover.

sun setting,
pupil dilated.

i must work.
i must finish.

still more.
until moon is
my only witness.

but i am still
digging.

predator's end of the gun   00

the glowing white
rage of that
passively unwanting
face,
a worn buddha
refusing to weep,
your eyes
defied me,
bolted,clamped
and locked from me
any perspective
of that pain
any symptom
of the injury
that chronicly
shown so acutely
in your uncurving
lip.

though at first
minutes earlier
you seemed
hostess friendly,
too pleasant.

then, i knew,
i was nowhere

near you.

pressing my fingers
between bone
within flesh just above
your heart
to resuscitate a part
that had no muscle,
that had no analogy
in anatomy.

but i could not
begin to imagine
or pretend
i understood,
the hostage-
held with-
cold barrel-
sociopath-
at other end
of gun-
sit and smile-
just accept it,
your role,
lay back
and
enjoy it-
it's the law of
the jungle

silence.

regarding
my warmest hand
coldly, guardingly,
as just another
seduction
another
invasion to innermost
avalon.

you gazed
as the raped do
gaping at the distance
within their eyes
toward a
imperceptible star,

as you
could not stop fingers
but
could refuse to feel.

that in
this rag-gagged
scream
your voice,
your objection
was muteness.

a reed
whose strength
was in snapping
in a river
unceasing,
unyielding.

but my hand
was shivering.

my own rage
that our fathers
put me here.

at the
predator's end
of the gun.

maelstroms 02

and the wind
made you.
currents of air,
sparkling of mist
condensed
your transience.
a face
so ancient
stone carved
with the dynamic
of your memory.
and the air
is a slow tempest
drawing you away
dissolving
to be remade
into another
configuration.

you could be a storm
violent
and
relentless
or you could be as fog
silence incarnate.

but always
some winged creature
arching over me
isolating myself
with my own thought
but
barely covering
that which was most
vulnerable.

we were as
cross currents
in the turbulent mirror,
two maelstroms
succumbing
to each other's
vacuum.

vestige of vestigial   00

and i remember
believing,breathing,
that i had to stop
to be good enough
for my unborn children.
that i had to die,
file down my claws,
stop bearing my jaws,
to repress that smile
that my darker
pushed through my skull.

a prey
deprived its right
of defense;
a hunting
making me so weary
of love
that i exhaust in the
demands of its presence.

for
i was pronounced
unhuman
barely from the womb.

in china
they drown me.

in arabia.
i am cloaked and shadowed.

in india
i am raped but untouchable.

and in jerusalem
i am the succubus
with an apple.

as a woman
it is not a matter
of destruction or not,

you will be.

of mutilated or not,
you are.

ask lilith,
ask sedna,
ask the fingers and the hands
their arms remember.

ask any shriek
that is called
a shrew.

no,
it is not a matter
of losing parts or not...

but which part.

which pound of flesh
will be extracted
for this most carnal sin
of birth.

which part
can you live without?

ophelia chose her mind,
and went mad.

joan chose her heart,
and was burned.

eve chose her womb,
and was damned.

i will choose
the only part
truly vestigial.

you.

mother's fear 00

she spoke
about a dream.

her hands
prying back
the boards,
the plaster,
the stray wires ,
hissing like a tangle
of adders
in a collapsed shelter.

pulling back
the savaged hair
from a wet swollen face.

too late.

even as the child
slept upon her lap.

her breath was panic,
her every motion
a shutter about to close.

as if the walls had heard her
as if this disaster would
play itself out behind them.

threatening to enter.

her frantic fingers
managed a stillness
to goad waking eyes to sleep

and to hold a cigarette
to her last horrible thought.

vine 00

```
              tree
                 dripping
                    woman
        shivering   in snow blissfully
      twisted spine          absymal   intertwined
      climbs this            in vines       in the dust
  whose chorus              victim       autumn leaves
  a congregation          of an        equations  whispering a previous  cellular
        of hands in    ecstatic  within pascal's      season of thought   contruct
          strangulation,   uncalculated          in its contours of     a pulse
                      essence,        the tender curve    without blood
                    frail, unspoken                    therefore
                                                    without end
                                                    a chaos
                                           entangling itself
                                           with order
                                           the memory
                                         of its other
                                         in its flower
                                           that drops
                                              with merciful


                                              gravity
            to the soil to dream in darkness of the sun.
```

the epilogue hiakus 00

c.t.
wonder child, blue eyes;
sky of private sculpted woods
birds wings, painters brush

s.b.
stick clicking blind with
hue of sunset voice sings
souls dimensions

c.d.
tao priest, quantum prayer
sublime smile orchestrating
his observations

r.s.
novice nomad knows
rain's whispers and snow secrets
lay in guitar strings

j.m.
fingers symphony
lifting her hair as wind-wild
gypsy violin

d.r.
hidden among grass
old man giving birth to
a river of thought

m.t.
a voice alighting
venus of true proportion
cathedral of sound

fathom 01

it is an emptier ocean
that knows it own
darkness

is not a choice,

but a
frenzied feeding
of its own children
upon itself.

no wonder it is silent.

its depths only amplify
that it would rather not
hear.

that it must
be the receptacle
for all that sun
refuses to see.

sea
only a mute
tight lipped
so that it will
not be asked
to swallow more.

the passenger 01

a car door
rattles the restlessness
of my last
kindly expecting nerve.
a sweating skin
waiting for a wind,
a taut conclave
of crimes;
the bleached bones
of all
the parts of me
i drove to the desert
in my trunk.

now casting a shadow
upon the passenger seat
of my car.

and she wants
the wheel.

for she demands
a confession,
a concession,
from the disallowed
that has replaced her
through a temporal
law of survival
of the amnesic.

only the quiet,
only the timid,
survive time;
meek mammals
holed in hollow
as the earth burns.

only the
pointlessly prolific
have had the
progeny alive today.

these knowings,
insects that hover
a mist of loudly-voiced
insignificance,
echo upon the
nautilus of my
inner ear
to mislead me
with a false sound of ocean.

as i try to hear
the silence sitting next to me,
directing me.

as the road,
remembers itself from the void.
just beyond the
stigmatism of my headlights.
only the wheels have faith,
only my passenger
my haunting victim,
knows the way.

she sits, hands folded;
a patient child
of a deeper current.
a mermaid
cursed with legs
that walked her to a death
pursuing the source
of the river.

i will try to return
her there.
to resolve her,
to dissolve her,
as foam upon the waves.

but if i cannot
reach the sea,
i will drive
into the desert.

let 01

i am
the madwoman
walking
into the tide.

i want
to close my eyes
and sink.

let the ocean
reclaim the salt
it has given me.
it has made little
palatable
upon my tongue.

let it rupture,
in it's pressured depths,
the cells
that have carried me,
this body, beyond
my will.
i am tired of
this weight
i want
to float
down.

until,

darkness
is my eyes,
silence
is my ears.
only the dull thumping
of this heartbeat
resounding
in this cocoon;

this black
more honest
than sun.

it tells me
only the dreams
i knew
before that star
ever touched me.

until,
i am the abyss.
full of my own need,
wordless
in my meaning

and i have
forgotten.

let me.

fugitive 01

and i walk
a wounded
faceless fugitive
among the buzzing
swarm of faces,

a murderer
counting upon
a crowd.
the indifferent
windows reflecting,
of all the eyes avoiding
mine
and their potential
dangers.

a distant radio.
a snatch of conversation.
a nearing siren.

they converge
in the loosening
of my mind.
i hide in
its pollution
of adrenalized limbs

its sound
drenches my clothes.

and
upon me,
the cacophony.

i walk too slow
in this to be innocent.
my guilt
a carefully calculated
calm.
too obvious.
but no one notices.

they walk slowly too.

and i spot a solace.
a wheeled womb.
pulling upon the car handle
i collapse within.

and now
the silence.
an insulation.

and i realize
that i'm taking
my first breath
in minutes,
in years.

it falls out
of me,
a confession
i no longer
have the strength
to carry.

staring out
the window

i let myself bleed.

four steps to goodbye 02

1.

and every hand
reminds me
of how close yours
once was.

you have stolen my words
and hidden them
in the wrinkles of the pillow
where so many unremembered
utterances still reside.
their shape echoes your lips.

and even in my sleep,
where you were once
so constant,
i can no longer hear them.

when dew was a diary,
when the sky was forgetful,
and
and this bed had no memory.

2.
let it fall.

do not grasp upon
that which
you reach for;

an uninterrupted gleam
you gazed as if
upon a lover
upon some unsatiated
loss of mother.

but it was upon
an empty corner
that your eyes
fell.

3.

split at the quadrants
an orange
before its ripening
but long after it's
consummation.

the succulent
made feculent.
i was merely debris

as you walked
with a purloined,
safe conscience,
yet
you embellished
each courtesy
with an implied accusation.

a word
rearing
like a predator at poise.

but i
answered with
a distance,
a birds wings
dreaming of wind

and i evaded you
with the tapestry
of flight.

i left you
clasping your hands.

4.
goodbye.

except the rain 02

the sun burns my skin,
the moon is eyes,
the clouds hide from me,
clarity;
all speaking in alien
languages.

except the rain.

the desert is my thirst,
the jungle my most primal fear,
the mountain humbles me,
humility;
all are habitats
inhospitable.

except the rain.

the snow wants sleep,
the wind demands i run,
the earth only swaddles me,
infancy;
but none will be my
companion

except the rain.

its rivulets   my veins
its current   my pulse
its salt   my taste
its maelstrom   my eye
i accept the rain.

of gods 02

chamunda was dancing
a skeleton
pregnant with
a primordial expanse of stars.
sanguine
dark luminous fluid,
the arms
of her many fingertips
prism cocoon
embracing,
bracing
the darkness.

a wound
that dissolves
as sand.

she
the unspoken,
frolicked
with kali,
the unheard.

arm in arm
pale sinuous creatures
singing beneath the moon,
an ancient orb
who hummed the rhythms
of their veins,
and slept
eyelid to eyelid
in the rain-swept foliage
of a disembodied kiss,
two winds intertwining.

forever and the end.
their twisted limbs divining
in their shapes;
their hungers feeding but
never satiating
each other.

two demons
whose atrocity
is only the fear
behind mortal eyes.

the dissection 02

the darkening
of your eye
dilates
in your dissection
of me.
a calculated, dissected,
barely taut
inflection of fingertip
pulling back my midsection
much as
the your least concerted,
breath upon
my name
billows back
the skin
of my strategies.

i calloused myself
to it
with practiced
self-infliction,
but the insinuated word
of your glance
cut through
my every sinew
dissolving it into
a gossamer
of interrupted thought
that
i grope
with my brow
and
scattering eyes
to somehow remember.

but scent of your voice
demands
another memory.

morning commute 02

speed
is another
form of rage.
a running,
a pursuit.

i blacken my eyes,
glistening and expressionless,
hiding in all the places
another driver
would expect to find
a human feeling,

but does not.

i will not give him
even a curve of lip,
even as i avoid
a reckless swerve
that just may soon
have a wreck.

a predator,
i have apparently
violated his territory
or maybe
he's just
trying to mount me.

or maybe
this nameless violence
is the last emotion
we worn-out monkeys
have for mating.

a mindless grip
upon our tools.

i smile.
it gives new meaning
to opposing thumbs.

salome 02

the sound of
a crevice
hiding within itself,
a congregated
whisper.

i disrobe,
i dance
upon the remnants
of the rain
arching through
its planes and angles
floating upon
its silences
and ruminations,

demanding my gift
from my present.

and with this
seduction
i toss aside
another
blinding veil.

never 02

never
is the only knife
that has the honesty
to cleanly dissect you.

eyes tremble
with an ache
as if loosening
themselves from drowning
in some near arriving
ocean
and years erode
and the shore retracts
from any obligation
to you.
now time to swim.

clay,
in every hand
their fingers
have shaped me
with hurtful
concavities
and
purposeless
bends.

i am
a sculpture
of all
they will never admit.

and i am hardening.

vision 00

the stone icons
floated
against the violet sky
of perpetual sunset.

their immovable lips,
uncarved
unspoken wisdom;
their rain degraded
crumbling marble
costumes
chiseled upon them
by our customs.

but
they were not trapped
by these trappings.

shivas
in eternal pose
of dance,

buddhas
arms gestured
in infinite blessing,

gargoyles
skulking wings
in poised alightment

through
these aged eyes

i could see
their enlightenment

and beneath them
i saw a landscape
of repression,

a sky too heavy
for the sun
to rise,
too asleep
to be awakened
for blue

and
a sideward growing
moss
that had intended
to be a tree.

the ritual 02

i so much feel
not long of
this earth,

a fading
shadow in
a doorway.

and this ache
a brier
that scratches my flesh
but is my only
outer form,

to the shivering
hunted ,hiding
within
with eyes
of the look
of a forgone conclusion

cutting,
razor
slicing canvases.

the crack of a match,
and just before the light
an inhale,
a deep slow vacuum,
nostrils curl upon
the smell of sulfur.

a latent moment.

then fibers char,
then glow,
then blow,
an ash,
a act
of self consummation.

meditating upon this
creative destruction
as if performing
a ceremony of
ritual sacrifice
intoxicated by the
incense
of my own
sweat and breathing.
but still,

an unchanged moment
no god answered.

the empath 02

opal,
curvature of moon.
its delicate line
the reminder
of fragile blue
shining in a sunrise
somewhere behind me.

even with this skin
upon me,
what i feel is not
always my own.
there are times
i sit quietly
in a smoke filled corner
of a room
of socially acceptable riots
of mating,
of hating,
this world of willful unknowing,

and i let them
write their stories
upon me,

but there are
some passages
i refuse to read.

others try
reading me
like a shakespearean sonnet;
perfections,
misdirections.

a delinquent
diagnosing
the disappeared.

the ocean can
swallow
only so much.

somnulent vigil   02

i'm thoughtful
about everything
because
i have thoughts
about nothing
.
my skin
is unable
to recognize itself
from the air,

and a beautifully
anguished voice
reminds me of one
i have left behind;

and its falling
from my own mouth.

this pain
is no pain.
it feels like desire
without a vein.

it falls and forms
rivulets and finds
crevices in me,
a rain in the desert,
somehow always
discovering
the hidden ocean
of forgotten storms.

it revives creatures
uncurling from
the barrenness
of the soil,

a wanting
in awakening
i am the shell
of that longing.

a landscape
wandering itself.

husk 02

a piece of child
you outgrew.
your mirrors,
your vanities,
for a reflection
for a world of larger ones.
your limbs
stretched and grew
the height of your wanting,
the depth of your need
you were soon
your own
antiquity.
an expectation
already filled
or
already failed upon.
a dream
too many times
woken within
and then forgotten.
a dust too many
times disrupted,
a husk collapsing
forgetting the shape
of the life
it once held.

predator 02

this horizon;
a lizard
with a desert
for a spine
but an unblinking
sunset
for an eye.
it stares
through
with prehistoric coldness
but somehow
warms me
with its indifference.

it does not hunt me
today.

the predator
that tracks me
is not so brave
as sky.

it is a thinking
cowardice
that knows
it vulnerability
more mortally
than my own.

prey 02

give me one wish.
pour plaster
into this fossil
and see if it takes.
what shape will it be?

human tenderness
has been ostracized.
at the edge
of the savannah
the predators
have been killing off
my weakest beliefs.
dragging gangly, tangled
long-legged limp
bodies into the bush.

the snapping
of bones cracking
crackles like a bonfire.
should i throw myself
upon it?

all that lives
wants to die

but the rest
runs like me,
a stream of sweat
and egoless cowardice.
a flight of many
small panics
eventually
tiring and settling
into a more quiet terror.
what will come next?

which of this
herd unheard
will be sweet, viscous salt
upon the teeth?
a fetus of a dream?
a wounded old wanting?

i will outrun this
until i am
a single thought
without even an echo
to follow it.

the last thought,
what shape will it be?

each street a memory,
shadows whose makers
have left to make more
apparitions
elsewhere.

it's like being
the last living thing
in a graveyard,

and somehow
the corpses are more alive.

just me and the sky.

outside the walls
and the ivy
in dim bedrooms
and
spasmodically lit
nightclubs,
bodies writhe
in death spins
their fingers,
their need
an attempt
to hold back mortality
yet
in their whispers
and
wordlessly articulate eyes,

am told that love exists.

am told
think too much upon things
cannot change.

am told that
simply did not try hard enough.
either way
it is always is and will be.
that

never understood
or did too well, that
was beaten down
or not beaten nearly enough.
all
know
is that my nights
are no longer sleepless.

they are dreamless.

a seamless
void.
if only my old nightmares
would wake me from this.
even hot and cold
eventually numb.

how many more days
will
relive realization
of all that
cannot prevent.

now
know what all
those dreams were about.

a warning...

blue 02

a blue
that held a black,
that held the stars,
that held the pupil,
of your eye;
that you held
with your multitude
of hands,
tendon ligament
construction
of your many
obligations,
of the loci,
of the thoughts
so equidistant
from each other.

your hands were
a radial spectrum,
you pulled each thread
and the room
unraveled.

yet with all this power
your arms still embraced
a void,
an empty,
that was the sole organ
of your body's function.
a moment
held in reverence
of the loneliness
of a lover someday returning.

the untouchable 02

maybe earth
will love me more.

absorbed
i will finally
have an embrace
that will not attempt
to comfort me
with lies,
with words;
thoughtless ramblings
spoken more from habit,
thought more from inheritance;
from lips who think
they know what mother is.

i am a child
and i will be childless.
it is the most maternal
thing to do.
i will drink no more,
i will not condemn another
to suckle upon the empty milk
of false assurances;
a breast that feeds
to fill its own hunger.
war cry
of both peri and pariah.
an ache escaping only
when the coroner
dissects me upon the table;
a whisper
as i leave
and it will travel
as all sounds;
into silence.

beyond your hands
i am
the untouchable.

maybe earth
will love me more.

disallowed 02

my feelings
only hurt me.

then i will be
what you want,
i will not feel.

and my love
only makes me hate,
for all that touched me
has only left bruises
and this is all
it ever intended

it's just the way
things are,

for i am disallowed
they will not
even grant the honesty
of forbidding me.
no chains
just a series of
locked doors
channeling me
into the desired
direction.

it's just the way
things have always been.

mother,
daughter,
prude,
prostitute.

all are only
synonyms
for slave.

so
i will not move.
i will lay upon the ground
until the wind takes me
as dust.

my womb unused,
my skin untouched,
my mind unspoken.

this love is numbing
in all it makes me feel.

the spell 02

a bud
upon my lips
blossoming
in my thought,

unfolding
that which seemed
so
inviolate,
violet
upon the green.

a hand
calloused ancient
conjuring
the crystalline wind,

you looked away
from your body
hoping
it would dissolve
sand in tide,
that somehow
you could erase
the fingers
that have touched you.

head held
in such martyred execution
in the skill
of blindness,
in the audacity
of sleep,

your lips
parted
in a prolonged silent
breath that would
never leave your lungs
yet somehow
pulled the rest of you
into disappearing,

a word
as bird
upon the blue.

moebeus 02

and without intrusion
you enter.

a hand quivering
upon my stomach,
a heart
reminding me of flesh.

in such intensities
you exist;
in subtlety
a distant piano,
a skeletal leaf
upon my window.
your pattern
disrupts mine
in my pursuit
of its understanding.

each thread follows
until
i am a knotted skein
folding
in such a way
that each moment
is the straightest
of lines to your eyes.

a critical mass
that makes me mute.

somehow you pull me
so far away
so as to lead me back
to myself.

small memory 02

i held up photographs
of a child
and asked you
who it was.

thinking her
some niece or cousin;
inquiring upon a
small memory
so i could interrupt
that stolid stare with a smile.

"it's me..."

it had an unexpected effect.
your receding eyes darkened
and a
slight tremor of resolve
spoke.
"...it *was* me..."

the smile
i received
was an orchestrated
nervously hardened
decoration.

this reflection
was a scorching.
you left in the pattern
of your silhouette
upon the wall;

a shadow believing itself
so far removed
from anything
living.

leper,
you tried
not to infect
anyone with
your lonely desires.

the devout gasp
of a name.

that i did not believe,
that i would not believe,
for i would not condemn you.

that cast me into the desert
and you
quickly recovered
like a sudden storm.

earth you are 02

and i was thinking
of how much like
earth you are.

brutal floods
preparing a soil for
gentle growth
softening rock to silt,
uprooting oak
for the
susceptible sapling,
a quake
a turning in your sleep
a stretching of a limb
that you execute slowly
to change your form.

shedding no tears
for the desert
knowing
that the rainforest
needs them more.

and your sun
has no favorite children
and your night
exposes all .

behind the swaddling
of blue sky,
to the void expanse
with only moon
as an echo of a
returning star.

you give me the silence
for my thoughts
to come home;
meandering nomads
seeking even
a transient permanence
to sleep

but leave me sleepless,

so even your absence
has presence with me.

my eye to star,
my back upon the grass.

i feel you turning
barely holding me
to ground,

so much
to me
earth you are.

09.12.01

the sky is ashen.
it is morning
and the blanket
is still upon me,
a quiet that encapsulates
my thoughts
into a small room
of whispers.
in this,as in any house,
the children awaken first
they question each other
in low voices;
with almost praying faces
the worries
that hide
when told to hush
by heavier footfalls.

ready for work.
another day. another day.

but for now
they hold this moment
suspended
between thumb
and forefinger,
detailing with their eyes,
testing with their attention,
the sharp unplayful edges
of a relic
carelessly left upon
the table.

09.11.02
a mark indelible, a word soundless.
i can feel you within my pulse
and just beyond my fingertips.

12:01 A.M. bourbon street 02

caverns of night
echo my laughter
at me.

young flesh
benevolent vampires
consuming.
pounding drums,
rhythms
pulse veins.
teeth of dull hostility
clenching with intent,
some young predator's
mauling claws,
mastering their
capacity for puncture

the song that split
the soul,
peeled it like an orange.
a child's expectation,
a singularity of soul.
aperture.
a crystalline shattering,
music as ice forming,
an infection
of temporary humanity,
of knowing

a warmth
that makes the hand
claw at its own heart
to satiate a need,
the fullness
that makes the hole

i want no cure.

let it spread.
pale and sweating
let me succumb
as dull flesh
to know this.

07.04.02

sparks floating,
a firecracker air,
a noise,
the night
an onset of turbulent
foliage
infinitely unfolding.

chaotic harmonies.

the glowing,
sprawling,
drunken sleep
upon a strangers eye
a somewhere, an everywhere
a voice
of forced birth words,
grasps
to the membrane of my intention,
the skin on the
back of the throat
and
every physical object
resists me.

but a sun spilling,
egg-thin translucence
whispers and stretches
across my ears,
the barely annunciated
pulse of my blood.
and quiet click and crack
of this voice,
the static of age and vinyl
speaks like a distant planet's
traces;

a last hand upon
the void.

good daughter 02

a paradigm
constricting
the contours
of conversation.

ever climbing, clinging
to the lobes of ears
the teeth demanding
the milk
from my unmaternal breast.
fingers forcing apart
my knees,
my needs,
an uncalculated variable
in an equation
making me null,
making me dull
to their needling
niceties.

and the shriveled husks
of humans
come to me for water.

the good daughter;
a sound that
stretches a closet
to a corridor.

if you kill me
you'd better hope
there's no such thing
as haunting.

seed 02

a dusklike dawn
upon
an unearthen beach,
a darkened watcher,
an interuption of wind,

she is the silohuette
of fugue
just awakening.

her fingertips
a retro-lapsed
raw tender
stroking,coaxing
of a violated shore.

down a silted strata,
a planet's repression,
her hands handling
the intangible,
the past's reprocussion
that is her,
the pulse ill earned
through birth.

and through the
choking unspoken
of her throat,
these layers
preach and pray
of the glistening
alien but mother
artifact
surrendered
to her trust
from burdened soil.

it has held this secret
too long.

exorcism 02

the voice that calmed me
humming inarticulate
in the walls aroun;
a consummating exhale
that felt like falling.

a tangling lace
like tides,
the unreachable line
of the ocean.

you're the slam of the door
at the end of the hall;
the talisman
that infects and protects,
branding my skin
with the words i never said
a wound of what i never did,
casting a lucid shadow
that speaks to me
while i am half asleep
at midnight,
a haunting.

the yawning
of a window
keeping me
at the farthest
corner.
as if your open
could
enclose me.
a snow drifting
into a frozen ocean,
a footstep
stopping upon
my stair;

i'm always waiting
for you,

a dream
treated
as prophecy
and followed
here.

it's time
i've forgotten
you.

encountered 02

it is inherent
in you
to smile,
to beguile
with an
ever exacerbating
eloquence,
elegance
a precision
that reduces me
seduces me.

eyes,
as slipping fingers,
you dropped below
my consciousness
losing hour of words
to your private alphabet

and even as
i sense you,

distant,

i am close enough
to be devoured,
disarmed enough
to be overpowered,

and even amnesic
i would know
the detail of even
your most subtle
expressions
as obsessions
stampede through
my most secluded
of sensual pleasures
leaving a wake
of obstruction
behind them.

an eggshell away
from realization.

my desire,
a fierce pulling
undercurrent
under the seemingly

still

gentle ripples of lake
as the
flicker of lash,
parting of an eye,
the near invisible
movement of a lip,
and
gesture of a hand,

only hint
of the raging dynamic
within.

the after 02

you seduced me
with the
exquisite clarity
of pain
in your face.

curved to the sky
as if praying,
close-eyed to mine
as if dying,

what was it
that made you bleed
so much
upon me
and still have
so strong a pulse?

as if loss
replenished,
as if grief
served a need,

just as the most
violent of storm
leaves both debris
and clear sky,

suckling upon
an unhappened moment
its image
scorched
upon your throat
leaving you
mute
for
some separate
temporal path untaken.

hostage 02

my red eyes
and sunset window
of heart,

it was purging.

your eye
a familiar pattern
of ecstatic dissection,
i fluttered
with its point
in me.

in this
vacuum of attention
i nodded passage
to passing silhouettes,

a feigned distraction
as i outran you,

awaiting
the slam of door
behind me.
still i heard
you slip in before it.

i turned.

you seem to have
nestled
somewhere within me,

a gentle refusal
to leave,
denying me
the privacy
of my lost hope
with your
needful eyes,

as if to complete me
with your
incompletion,
and this warm
was new on me

so i did not shiver,
so i could sleep,
as i once had
without fitful dreams;

a willing hostage
kidnapped from my
own ransom.

establishing dominance 02

a philosophy
handed down
father to son to father
like a broken old watch
that doesn't know
what time it is.

you quiet me
forcibly
with the boom
of your voice,
but
the silence
has more intelligent
things to say.
all this
wailing, ailing
an alien fiddle
and the strum
of strings
and pounding of drum
resonates
as the sunrise
of a rising wind.

your emptiness
regards
consummation
with me
as an actual
act of feeding.
your conquests
the measure
of your private
failure.

reincarnated 02

implosion,
unable to sustain
a singularity's hunger

but even
upon collapse

a mirror of construction
is born:

the instant reversal
of every futile
despairing
belief that had
been killing you.

some destruction,

some ancient
laying unraveled,
a primordial
truth traveled,

a bloated
inflammation
of virus
larvae chewing
upon the dead.

if only i could hold onto
this clarity,
this buddha of being
this soft
unjudgemental god
smile,
the blissfully
superannuated
mortal strolling
a inch above the ground
forgetful of even gravity.

as a breathed sigh
of the buried,
of the drowning,
at last
accepting
even that which
takes them.

up from the
Dark Ocean
i rise
my lungs full
of the swallowed
night
that i will speak
upon the sun.

rising memory 01

i collapsed
some primal
purge of pain.

it came.

you had held
some risk
of unknowing;

her.
you told her
what it took me
26 years to hear.

and somehow
it reached
back to
that even now
forgotten
moment,

when she had
closed her eyes.

it was like
forgiving
and being
forgiven

for some
lost humanity,

for a murder.

that i know
now,
despite
asphyxiation,

her small hands
had held onto me.

even with her
muffled voice,
my every lethal
intention,

i was still terrified.

as if her tenderness
would destroy me.

O.b.^E. 02

and the
tenuous expanse
widening within
my stomach,
with
its saturated void,
its dim distant stars,
burning my eyes
to tears

as the silence
of infinity,
the thin paper
sheer veil
hums a memory
of a womb heartbeat.

and this body
has a weight
beyond that of gravity.

i feel the earth
fragile orb
spinning, weaving
a mere millennium
in the moment,
a foster parent
to a stray
runaway
child;

a homesickness
felt but not understood.
a life of faces,
intimates
now nameless,
participants
in a vague dream,
a dimensionless
projection
upon the depth of time.

i have forgotten.

the sleep disrupted
by a voice without
words
that does not pulsate
the sludge thickness of air
but resonates
the slickness of ice.

an aperture of soul
that makes thought and
memory meaningless

i have not forgotten.

i have awoken from
the dream
or the dreamer
has awoken me.

two entities one eye
and all is time.

waking 02

behind my pain
is my desire.

a membrane
of kin,
of skin,
of flesh
that both
protects
my soul
and guarantees
my mortality.

within
a landscape
with its span,
it has exquisite scarcity,
in the glistening of its night
inhabitants
and the presence of creatures
scarred by atrocity.

there is
a world in me
stretching
a womb in me
germinating
that which will
never grow in the sun,

but
beneath a dim blue star
of a twilight planet,
seen only upon
my eyelids,
felt only behind
my fingertips,
(but not upon them)

it is waking,
opening
as a lily
for rain.

skewed 03

a trauma
is always
reruns
& repetitions.

the rocking of
the wailing;
history's chain
of tyrants.
and
how this always
returns
to your refusal.

numb
from the waist
                    down,
                drugged
        from the neck up,
                    and
                hating
everywhere in between.

                only my legs
                    recollect
                the miles
            in their want
            for collapse.

                but i stand.

damned 03

in the low drowning
of his voice,
i could almost hear
the weights
hunching his shoulders,
drawing his eyes
downward in
some inherent shame,
some impending punishment.

"i will find some truth in this. . . "

the tenuous membrane
of his face
over-filled with an
unbearable solution
that his eyes
barely kept
dammed,
damned.
it was a word
foolish priests have
for heathens
but behind his pressed lips
it was a resolution.

". . .just face it . . . "

a child
held at gunpoint
behind his face,
buried small fingers
grasping up through soil
only to be shoveled in
by a shake of
his head.

". . . i failed. . ."

he fed it
forcing down food
out of habit
not desire
and
strategically scheduling
his attention
in the smooth
concise precision
in which he
finally smiled.

"it's o.k."

through the window,
the sun
reminded his skin
of a distant summer.

01.01.03

and i have
awoken.

a gray
with walls
and a barely dressed
bed.
in the nightstand,
in the corner of
the drawer,
a huddling
of my semi-precious
belongings.
the rings, necklaces,
and i wonder
why these?
is this all i have left
to rescue?

for i am in
a haunted house,
a dust about
to collapse upon itself,
and i must leave.
i traverse a darkened
staircase.
this child is no longer
afraid.
it would have me
butchered
or
one of its ghosts.
and one waits for me.
an old woman
in the doorway.
at the bottom of
stairs.

is she is
my guide
or
my gallows?

01.19.03

joy is a skill
that children do not create
but learn
and reflect.

is this twilight,
this quiet lightning,
a reminder
upon my throat
to feel?

a familiar chorus
hummed
upon a younger voice
than mine.

it's my birthday,
i've blown out candles
and unwrapped presents.
and for all the family
here,

there
is a silence at
the end of the table.

it watches,
it smiles
invisibly nodding
upon what she sees.

telling me
that i'm not so far
that she cannot see me.

and that this
is not
a futile celebration.

and her breath
is the one
that fills me
for this wish.

the modern poet 03

my breath
is a crack,
on a cackle,
on a scream.

the road is hesitant
again this morning;
slow pulses
of people in shiny capsules,
husks within husks.

i growl
earthily a clear bandwidth
of obscenities.
my own capsule
keeps me politely quieted
behind glass.

to sight
i am terrorist scribbling a manifesto
but
i am the picture of a modern poet.
(though i doubt many discern the two)

my rumbling engine
quakes the hand
now writing upon this pamphlet
that reads::
"mental health associates
psychological services
to the south shore community".

inside is comfort
to the drunken or damaged.
phone numbers of even more people
with strategies you've already tried,
in the end,
telling you to be chemically lobotomized
at the hands of the unqualified.

just to stop you from complaining

after all, it's so depressing.

damaged 03

exhausted
with ourselves,
we looked upon
each other
with a distant wonder;
a negligible fascination
as if studying
the cracks in a broken pavement
and
finding an expression
that matched our own.

a blade of grass
that somehow always
finds the place to grow,

hope is a weed
that brings despair
in its flower
and
and resolve
in its
regenerating
seed.

survival of
the most unfit,
the most damaged.

misshapen 03

"i am mutated
in a way
that my body
only hints upon"

i never saw
an eye so
coiled from itself,
recoiled
at the prospect
of it's own beauty.

as if it was
easier to believe
blindness,
that black
an inanswering mirror
to your doubts.

as if tenderness
was too treacherous
a liability
for you to afford yourself,

a misstep
that could get you
killed.

such a failed
human being,

your sentences ran backward
until wordless
in the origin
of a thought

with a unique
perspective upon
the misshapen.

a shattering of windows,
a beautifully gutted architecture,
as your gasps of breath
is your body
struggling to keep your soul alive;
a changling
of missing parts
shreds and scatterings
of that
which was never whole.

mantra 03

hand upon my head,
i tremble
as if in an attempted healing.

i will try to be as saint
to myself
but all i ever manage
is to be an
hollow passage
of over rehearsed words.

a meaningless mantra.

"stop stop stop stop . . . "

as if
peace or epiphany
can be had
if i just plug my ears
with a repeated thought.

as if
my words
were miles i could
put between
myself
and
all that i remember.

as if, as if ,
always
as if
and never actual.

almost
as if
this just might

end.

www.ingramcontent.com/pod-product-compliance
Lightning Source LLC
Chambersburg PA
CBHW052105090426
42741CB00009B/1687